Gillian Porter Ladousse

Penguin Quick Guides Series Editors:
Andy Hopkins and Jocelyn Potter

PENGUIN ENGLISH

Pearson Education Limited
Edinburgh Gate
Harlow
Essex CM20 2JE, England
and Associated Companies throughout the world.

ISBN 0 582 46890 6

First published 2001
Copyright © Gillian Porter Ladousse 2001

The moral right of the author has been asserted.

Produced for the publisher by Bluestone Press, Charlbury, UK.
Designed and typeset by White Horse Graphics, Charlbury, UK.
Illustrations by Anthony Maher (Graham-Cameron Illustration).
Photography by Patrick Ellis.
Printed and bound in Denmark by Norhaven A/S, Viborg.

مال، دیوید
(ریلی یوزفول اینکلیش وربز) .
Really useful English verbs/ David Maule;
editors Andy Hopkins and Jocelyn Potter.-
تهران: صدف سماء، ۱۳۸۱ = ۲۰۰۲م
۱۶۰ ص: مصور. —. (Penguin quick guides)
انگلیسی.
فهرست‌نویس براساس اطلاعات فیپا.
افست از روی چاپ ۲۰۰۱: هارلو.
نمایه.
۱.زبان انگلیسی -- واژگان -- راهنمای آموزشی
(متوسطه). ۲.زبان انگلیسی -- اصطلاحها و تعبیرها
-- راهنمای آموزشی (متوسطه). الف.عنوان.
Really useful English verbs

PE۱۴۴۹/م۲ل۹
الف۱۳۸۱

۴۲۸/۱

کتابخانه ملی ایران

۸۱-۱۸۷۱۹م

Maule, David

انتشارات صدف سماء

Really Useful
English Verbs

چاپ : اول
تیراژ : ۵۰۰۰
لیتوگرافی : فام
قیمت : ۴۰۰ تومان

مرکز پخش : ۶۴۰۳۵۱۶ - ۰۹۱۱۲۷۲۱۶۴۷

Contents

Getting started

How can this book help you?

Do you want to learn more English verbs?
Can you say some of what you want to say but
not all of it, because you don't know the right
verb? Do you wonder where you can find the
verbs you need? The *Penguin Quick Guide to
Really Useful English Verbs* gives you the verbs
that you're looking for.

What's in this book?

There are over 200 really useful English verbs.
Each chapter looks at a different area of real life
– for example, jobs or travel. At the end of
every chapter you'll find exercises in the
Review section to help you remember what

you've learned. And you can check your answers at the back of the book. All the verbs in the book are also listed in the **Index**.

Why is this book called a *Quick Guide*?

Because it takes you straight to the verbs you need. For instance, perhaps you're thinking of working in an English-speaking country. So why not turn to chapter 4, *At Work*, on page 47? Here you will find lots of verbs that you will find very useful when applying for a job or in the workplace.

This is a *Quick Guide*. You don't need to spend hours studying it. Just open it for ten minutes every day – and see how quickly you learn.

- Choose a subject that interests you. Maybe you're sitting in a car, or on a train or a plane. Look at *Travel*, starting on page 23. Read the chapter and find verbs that go with what you're doing.

- Answer the questions in the **Review** section at the end. Then go to the **Answers** section at the back of the book. Were you right?

- Now go to the **Index**. Read the sample sentences – and write down the words in your own language.

I hope you enjoy using the book. Good luck.

Life!

1

Birth

Peter and Sally Greenwood

wish to **announce** the birth of their baby daughter

Melanie

on 7th September.

Mother and baby are doing well.

wish

announce

name

gain

A: We **named** her after her great-great-grandmother Melanie …

B: She's **gaining** weight nicely!

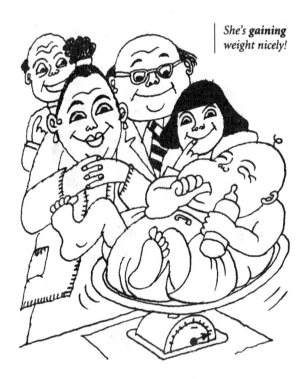

*She's **gaining** weight nicely!*

Birthdays

But my birthday was six months ago!

Dear Virginia ...

My boyfriend **forgot** my birthday again this year. He forgets it every year. He says he's sorry, and he didn't **realise** it was so important to me. He says he will **remember** next year. But he says that every year. I don't **believe** him any more. Someone who forgets your birthday doesn't really **care** about you.

forget

realise

remember

believe

care

Happily married

marry
decide
argue
agree
talk

Peter and I have been **married** for five years and we're very happy. We get on very well – we always have. We **decide** on everything together. We never **argue** about anything.
We **agree** on everything.
I know exactly what he thinks on any subject. In fact we don't really **talk** at all.

*In fact we don't really **talk** at all.*

Crystal ball

MAN: So tell me ... what can you see?

WOMAN: I can see a good life. Your financial situation will **improve**. Your career is already very successful, and it will **continue** to **develop** well. You will **earn** millions of dollars. You will travel a lot in the next twelve months and you will meet the woman of your dreams ...

improve
continue
develop
earn
give

*Why do fortune tellers only ever **give** you the good news!*

Final adventure

AAAAAAAGH!

At least he didn't suffer!

Mike Kane – a life of danger

Mike Kane, the well-known media personality, **survived** many adventures. He **led** an exciting life. He liked fast cars. He broke world records in his speedboat. He **met** a lion face-to-face in Africa. But yesterday he **fell** to his death from a hot-air balloon. It was very sudden. But at least he didn't **suffer**.

survive

lead

meet

fall

suffer

Review 1

A Put the verbs in the sentences.

agree suffer believe forget gain

1 The letter didn't arrive because I .... to send it.
2 We couldn't .... which car to buy.
3 I eat too much so I've .... weight.
4 He had painkillers so he didn't ....
5 He often lies so don't .... him.

B Replace the words in italics with a verb.

improve fall meet wish decide

1 I *want* to make a complaint.
2 I couldn't *make up my mind*.
3 Sales *went up* last year.
4 Profits have *gone down*.
5 I *was introduced to* Kathy last week.

Travel

2

Holiday plans

mind

visit

travel

lie

stay

SALLY: Where shall we go for our holiday this year?

DAVE: I don't **mind**. But I'm not **visiting** any more ruins.

SALLY: And I'm not **travelling** 3,000 miles just to **lie** on a beach somewhere.

DAVE: Well, if we can't agree, we can always **stay** at home.

We can always **stay** at home!

Weekend away

They call this travelling in style?

Travel in Style

Fly supersonic executive jet to New York. Stay at the five-star Grand Hotel. **See** New York from the air on our helicopter excursion, or if you **prefer**, take our cruise round Manhattan. **Enjoy** *Phantom of the Opera* on Broadway.

Return to London – flight arrives at Heathrow at 7.30 pm

Inclusive cost: only £4,999.

fly

see

prefer

enjoy

return

Travel advice

*I thought it said **ride** a camel in the brochure.*

WOMAN: We **want** to go on an adventure holiday. What can you **suggest**?

MAN: Well, there are a lot of possibilities. Let me **show** you some of our brochures.
Let's see. *See the Andes from the Patagonia Express, trek in the Himalayas,* **ride** *a camel in the Atlas mountains …*

WOMAN: Ah, riding a camel in the Atlas mountains, that **sounds** nice.

want

suggest

show

ride

sound

In flight

We have a 100% safety record on our flights.

Please **listen** to our safety demonstration.

You will **find** a life jacket under your seat. Do not **remove** it until the cabin crew tells you to. During the flight, please **keep** your seat belt on if you do not have to move around the plane.

In case of emergency, **follow** the floor lighting to the nearest exit.

listen

find

remove

keep

follow

Postcard

*The local people **welcomed** us warmly.*

POSTCARD

Thanks for taking us to the
airport. We **waited** and waited at
Heathrow. In the end we **left** four
hours late! Finally **arrived** safely.

The hotel is lovely. The local
people **welcomed** us very warmly.
They have a tradition here to
welcome tourists with tomatoes!

Will **write** again soon.

Love

Molly and Bill

wait
leave
arrive
welcome
write

Review 2

A Which verb goes with which noun?

1 ride   a) a plane
2 fly   b) a postcard
3 enjoy   c) a museum
4 write   d) a horse
5 visit   e) a holiday

B Fill in the missing verbs.

keep   travel   lie

1 I love to …. on a beach in the sun.
2 Please …. your safety belt on.
3 He's …. all over the world.

C Respond to this question in three ways.

Where shall we eat – the Brasserie or the Bistro?

1 (mind)   ....
2 (prefer) ....
3 (suggest) ....

Shopping

3

Nightmare

What about this one, madam?

ASSISTANT: Can I help you, madam?

WOMAN: Yes, I **need** something to **wear** to a wedding …

Later …

WOMAN: I don't know what to **choose**!

ASSISTANT: What about this one, madam?

WOMAN: It's pink, and pink doesn't **suit** me. Isn't there another colour?

ASSISTANT: Yes, we have it in green, madam. But it's not your size. I don't think it'll **fit** you.

need

wear

choose

suit

fit

Special offers

*Just think what we **saved** today!*

Compare our prices!
Superbrand products
cost less!

Save £££££££s!
Buy today. Special offers.

We're **closing**!
Clearance sale.
Last few days.

Spend now! Save later!

compare

cost

save

close

spend

Shoplifter

*Somebody must have **put** them there!*

GUARD: Excuse me, madam. Can I see your receipt?

WOMAN: Receipt? What do you **mean** receipt? I didn't **buy** anything. I was just **looking**.

GUARD: Then you won't mind if I just look in your bag, will you? …
What's all this, madam?

WOMAN: I don't know what they're doing there. I've never seen them before. Somebody must have **put** them there!

mean
buy
look
put

Internet shopping

A: I have to buy a present for Julie. But I **hate** shopping.

B: Then let's **try** the Internet. There's an e-arcade that **sells** everything you could want. We just need to look at their web pages. Here we are.

A: OK. I know, I'll **order** some perfume. It'll be here tomorrow!

B: Just fill in the details, then **pay**. Use your credit card.

A: But I haven't got a credit card!

hate

try

sell

order

pay

Complaint

Dear Sir,

I am writing to **complain** about your Oxford Street shop. I bought a shirt there on Monday. When I got home, I **noticed** it had a big stain. I **returned** to the store on Tuesday, and **asked** for a refund. The shop assistant **refused** and was extremely rude. I asked to see the manager, but he was not available ...

complain
notice
return
ask
refuse

Review 3

A Replace the words in italics with a verb.

cost   try   refuse   fit

1 This coat *is too big*.
2 This holiday *was* a lot of money.
3 We *used* a new supplier.
4 Never *say 'no'* to an offer of help.

B Put the verbs in the sentences.

save   spend   complain   pay

1 We .... about the bad service.
2 I went shopping and .... a fortune!
3 Do not .... by credit card on the Internet
   without a special code.
4 It's a good idea to .... some of your salary
   every month.

At work

4

Phone call

She's gone away …

MAN: Can I **speak** to Anna Grant?

WOMAN: Who's **calling**, please?

MAN: This is Bill Grant, her husband.

WOMAN: **Hold** the line a moment please, Mr Smith.

Later …

WOMAN: Mr Grant? I'm afraid Mrs Grant's not here.

MAN: Oh. When do you **expect** her back?

WOMAN: I'm not sure, Mr Grant. Her secretary tells me she's **gone** away …

speak
call
hold
expect
go

Office equipment

*I've **explained** how to **use** the photocopier ten times and he still doesn't **understand**!*

How to **use** the photocopier

Place the paper to be photocopied on the glass window.

Check that it is in the top right-hand corner.

Press the green button.

use

place

check

explain

understand

Changing jobs

A: You **seem** happy!

B: I am happy! I'm **changing** my job.

A: But you only **began** here last month.

B: Yes, but I've been **offered** a much better job. A huge salary, bonuses, a company car, 12 weeks' holiday.

A: That sounds good.

B: Yes, it sounds like paradise. There's only one thing wrong. It's in Antarctica!

seem

change

begin

offer

Job advert

We **require** a

DYNAMIC YOUNG EXECUTIVE

to **manage** an energetic sales team.

If you are looking for a challenge, we **invite** you to **apply** for this exciting opportunity and **become** a member of our unusual organisation.

We sell sand. We're looking for a new manager for our Middle East operation.

Job reference

She is very interested in a career in finance.

To whom it may concern

Bronwen Muller has **worked** in our accounts department for the last six months. As her supervisor, I have been able to **observe** her closely. She **learns** fast and has made good progress. She **obtained** her Advanced Accounting Diploma with Distinction while she was working here. She is very interested in a career in finance, and we **regard** her very highly.

work

observe

learn

obtain

regard

Review 4

A Fill the gaps with correct verb forms.

understand   expect   obtain   invite   check

1 I'll just .... the figures.
2 We .... him back any minute now.
3 I wasn't .... to the party.
4 She didn't .... the instructions, so she failed the test.
5 She .... her MBA from Oxford.

B Match the verb to the noun.

1 work   a) £60,000 per annum
2 hold   b) an eight-hour day
3 offer   c) a language
4 speak to   d) the line
5 learn   e) the manager

Company
Business

5

Annual report

Production at Wonder Goods Inc. has **increased** steadily over the past five years. Sales have gone up by 30% in that time.

We are **opening** three new factories next year. We **produced** a record 600,000 software packages last year.

Last year we **created** 2,000 jobs. All our employees are happy. They never **demand** more money. They never **strike** …

increase

open

produce

create

demand

strike

Reorganisation

Yes, that just leaves you and me and the company bank account!

A: Let's **discuss** the plans for the reorganisation.

B: Well, first we'll **cut** costs.

A: Yes, and **reduce** the number of workers.

B: That's right – **employ** fewer people.

A: Yes, so we can **avoid** paying all those salaries.

B: And we could get rid of the other partners.

A: Great idea! That just leaves you and me and the company bank account!

discuss
cut
reduce
employ
avoid

Sales plan

Homework4you.com

...homework
answers
for
schoolkids

We'll **provide** a valuable service to schoolkids everywhere!

JAKE: So how shall we do this?

JOAN: We'll **present** our new sales plans to the board of management. Jake, you're the sales director. You **introduce** our plans. Then we'll discuss them in detail with the board. I **hope** we can **reach** a satisfactory conclusion. The company must decide to **adopt** the project. After all, we will **provide** a valuable service to the consumer.

present
introduce
hope
reach
adopt
provide

Meetings

GUIDELINES FOR EFFECTIVE MEETINGS

prepare

read

answer

stick

express

- **Prepare** the meeting and **read** carefully any papers which are sent to you.

- Make sure you can **answer** any question that anyone might ask.

- **Stick** to the point.

- **Express** an interest in other people's views, even if you do not agree with them.

- Make positive contributions.

Advertising slogans

You know, something like 'Buy FIZZ!'

GAIL: I **say** 'Buy FIZZ!' It's short and snappy.

GUY: Boring!

GAIL: Well, what about: 'Our amazing new FIZZ **enables** you to **achieve** twice as much in half the time.'

GUY: No. Too complicated.

GAIL: What about: 'With new FIZZ we **aim** to cut your work by half!'

GUY: Too long!

GAIL: Well, you suggest something.

GUY: What about something short and snappy? You know, something like 'Buy FIZZ!'

say

enable

achieve

aim

Review 5

A Complete the text with these verbs.

employ aim increase reach produce

Our company [1].... 600 people. We [2].... 600,000 cars last year and our profits [3].... by 10%. We [4].... to [5].... an annual production of 1 million in five years' time.

B Fill the gaps with the correct verbs.

express discuss answer ask say

1 Dad, can I go out? Please .... yes.
2 The Company Director never .... his opinion.
3 Can I .... a question?
4 I'm afraid I can't .... that question.
5 Let's .... these problems calmly.

On the road

6

Lost!

*You **walk** along the main road …*

A: Can you tell me the way to the station, please?

B: Yes, of course. You **walk** along the main road for 200 metres. Then you **turn** left. You come to another road. You **cross** it, and then go straight on. The station is the second building on the right. You can't **miss** it.

A: Walk along the main road, turn right ... ?

B: No, no. Here, let me **draw** you a map.

walk

turn

cross

miss

draw

Driving home

It doesn't *matter* — we can *claim* it on the insurance!

A: What's the matter? You look terrible!

B: I left work half an hour ago. I **drove** home with Bill. He drives like a maniac. He **failed** his driving test seven times.

A: Seven times?

B: Yes, he only just **passed** it at the eighth attempt. I'm not surprised. He drove straight into some market stalls the other day – it was a miracle that nobody was hurt. And do you know what he said? 'It doesn't **matter** – we can **claim** it on the insurance!'

drive
fail
pass
matter
claim

Breakdown

I said **release** the clutch!

A: Oh no, the car won't start. I forgot to **replace** the battery.

B: Shall I get out and **push**? We can start it like that.

A: I hate to ask you, but yes ... No, wait a minute. You sit in the driving seat and <u>I'll</u> push.

B: Do you think I **can**?

A: Yes, yes, it's easy. You put the car in second gear, and then **release** the clutch when I tell you ...

replace

push

can

release

Traffic jam

*When do they ever **finish**?*

JOHN: At least we're **moving**.

MARK: Do you call this moving?
At ten miles an hour?

Later ...

JOHN: Look – the traffic has
stopped again.

MARK: I **wonder** what's **happened**
this time.

JOHN: Road works again, I expect.

MARK: I thought they'd **finished**.

JOHN: When do they ever finish
road works?

move
stop
wonder
happen
finish

Speedy transport

deal
collect
deliver
depend
supply
complete

SPEEDY TRANSPORT deals with customers all over the world.

We **collect** and **deliver** in record time – anything, anywhere. Our very competitive prices **depend** on the size of the package and the destination. We **supply** an estimate on request.

Simply **complete** the form below.

*Don't worry, we can **deliver** anything, anywhere.*

Review 6

A Which verb is different?

1 walk   stop   drive   move
2 deal   wonder   arrange   supply

B Fill the gaps with the correct verbs.

happen   miss   replace   depend   wonder

1 What .... ? You look terrible!
2 I .... where Bob is?
3 I'm not sure if I'll take that job. It .... on the salary.
4 We'll .... the train if we don't hurry.
5 If you leave, they won't .... you with someone else.

Fit and healthy

7

Health club

prove
smile
laugh
start

SMILING IS GOOD FOR YOU

It has been scientifically **proved**. Laughing is even better. Do you **smile** or **laugh** at least ten minutes a day? If not, come to our Health Club and follow our special fitness and health programme.

Start today!

Smile for at least ten minutes a day!

Gym club

	IAN: You could easily **lose** five kilos if you **joined** the gym.
lose	ALAN: What do you do there?
join	
run	IAN: An exercise routine. And then I **run** on the treadmill quite a lot, but I also **lift** weights.
lift	
drop	ALAN: I wouldn't like that. I'd be worried about **dropping** them!

I'd be worried about **dropping** them.

In training

You never know what's going to happen.

BILL: So Steve, tell us how things are going, as we get near the Olympics. Is the team going to **win**? Are you going to **break** a world record this year?

STEVE: Well, Bill, we're **training** hard every day. We'll do our best to **beat** our own record and **bring** the gold medal home. But nothing is certain. You never know what's going to happen.

win
break
train
beat
bring

Prevention

Be a good example to your children.

Prevention is better than cure

How can we **prevent** young people starting to take drugs? Here's some simple advice.

- **Ensure** young people understand the dangers of taking drugs.
- Keep talking to them.
- Be a good example to your children.
- Make sure relationships with parents are **built** on trust.
- **Encourage** children to develop healthy interests, like sport, right from the start.

prevent

ensure

build

encourage

Sun

cause

protect

control

add

include

SunStop

Everyone knows the sun's rays **cause** damage to the skin.

Too much sun can be dangerous. New SunStop **protects** you.

Control your tanning the sensible way. **Add** SunStop to your shopping list today, and make sure you **include** it in your holiday packing.

Too much sun can be dangerous.

Review 7

A What's the 'opposite' meaning?

prevent drop start laugh lose

1 She *won* the race.
2 He *lifted* the vase.
3 She *caused* an accident.
4 They *cried* all through the film.
5 He *stopped* the machine.

B Fill the gaps with correct verb forms.

add run encourage include smile

1 Now let's take this photo. ..... everyone, please.
2 If you .... 63 and 39, you get 102.
3 Have you .... the service in the bill?
4 The crowd .... the home team.
5 I never .... to catch a bus!

Law and order

8

Bank robbery

SLIPPERY JOE IN COURT

A man known as Slippery Joe appeared in court yesterday. He was **accused** of taking part in a bank robbery.

He was **caught** trying to get on a ferry to France with a suitcase full of cash. Joe **admitted** he had been near the bank at the time of the robbery, but **denied** taking part in it.

accuse

catch

admit

deny

White-collar crime

Crime Report

Police statistics **reflect** a growing trend as more white-collar crime is **committed** every day. Most white-collar crime involves **cheating** the system. Police need to become more expert in this kind of crime and are **attending** courses where they are **taught** about computer fraud and financial scams.

reflect

commit

cheat

attend

teach

Contracts

*Just **sign** the contract and **send** it back.*

MAN: I'd like to **thank** you for all your help.

LAWYER: Don't **mention** it!

MAN: I've read the contract. Most of it seems OK. I've just one query. It says 'I agree to pay Cruella Grimes £60,000 for services rendered.' Who is Cruella Grimes? And what are the services rendered?

LAWYER: Oh, don't **worry** about that. Just **sign** the contract and **send** it back.

thank
mention
worry
sign
send

Police warning

receive
identify
open
examine
warn

POLICE NOTICE

Terrorists can go to a lot of trouble with their parcel bombs. If you **receive** a package which looks suspicious, or if you cannot **identify** the sender, do not **open** it. It may be a bomb.

Call the police and wait for them to **examine** the parcel.

You have been **warned**.

Bag-snatcher

Did I hear right? Your pet snake?

WOMAN: Excuse me, officer. I'd like to **report** a theft. I was **standing** in the queue for the cinema. I was **carrying** my bag on my shoulder. This young man ran past. He **grabbed** my bag and ran off. It all happened so fast.

OFFICER: I see. What was in it, madam? Your wallet? Your driving licence?

WOMAN: No, no, no. It was my pet snake.

OFFICER: Did I **hear** right? Your pet snake?

report
stand
carry
grab
hear

Review 8

A Replace the words in italics with a verb.

attend   worry   admit   sign   deny

1 He *said* he was guilty of the crime.
2 She *said* the facts were *not* true.
3 We *were at* the meeting.
4 I *wrote my signature* on the contract.
5 They *were anxious* when their guests did not arrive on time.

B Put the verbs in the sentences.

warn   hear   catch   receive

1 We .... you that part of town was dangerous.
2 He .... an enormous fish.
3 She .... a medal for her brave action.
4 They could .... someone shouting.

Show
business

9

Hollywood

Ninety-three? I thought she was getting a bit old to be in Beachwatch!

OBITUARY

Mary Hadley

Hollywood star Mary Hadley **died** peacefully at her home late last night. She was 93. Ms Hadley **appeared** in many films and was **awarded** an Oscar for her performance in *Run for Your Life*. She **starred** with Carlo Haddon and many other of our favourite heroes. Her career lasted well over 60 years.

die

appear

award

star

Fame

discover

make

act

end

recognise

Michael Spain was **discovered** when he was only seventeen. He **made** his debut in the Hollywood success *Fast!* in which he **acted** superbly. He then rose to fame in a meteoric career which **ended** when he decided to become a Buddhist monk. He continues to be **recognised** in the streets by many who still want his autograph.

No, no,
I'm not
acting!

Don Quixote

... the most realistic stage horse I have ever seen.

At The Theatre

The magnificent set was **designed** by Spanish stage designer, Pedro Sanchez.

The curtain **rose** and **revealed** his dramatic set. Giant windmills were turning madly in the wind.

The audience was still gasping with delight when Don Quixote **entered** from the left on the most realistic stage horse I have ever seen.

design

rise

reveal

enter

Pop star

In the morning I always feel ready to move on.

I **loved** every minute of our six-month world tour. We **recorded** several concerts live, and I **know** we'll sell millions of the discs to all the fans who couldn't get to the concerts. And I know it sounds strange, but I actually **like** staying in a different hotel every night. But more than one night's a bit boring … in the morning I always **feel** ready to move on.

love

record

know

like

feel

Interview

So your book is **based** on reality?

HOST: Welcome to the show, Barbara Hughes. Now you've just **published** your tenth novel. I think it's wonderful that all your writing is so honest – and always **based on** reality. I get tired of reading those strange books where you have to **imagine** situations – situations that are, let's **face** it, quite impossible. Now … tell us about your book.

publish
base on
imagine
face

BARBARA: Er … you have read it, haven't you?

Review 9

A Complete the text with these verbs.

end make discover imagine die

I ¹.... a scenario about the year 2050. Scientists
².... the secret of eternal life. Nobody ³.... any
more. The story ⁴.... when there are so many
people on the planet, nobody can move. But
nobody wants to ⁵.... the film.

B Replace the words in italics with a verb.

recognise enter star award act

1 They *gave* him an Oscar.
2 The actor *came onto the stage* from the left.
3 She *plays the part* in a very dramatic way.
4 I *knew it was* Sarah immediately.
5 He *has the main part* in the film.

Power
verbs

10

Power Verb 1

Have

- HAVE can be a main verb. See the table opposite.

- HAVE can also be an auxiliary verb. It is usually used in perfect tenses.

I haven't seen Bill today.
He had never been to Nepal.

 British/US differences
I have (got) a car. (Br)
I have a car. (US)

I haven't seen him yet. (Br)
I didn't see him yet. (US)

Use/meaning	Example
ACTIONS	*She had a shower.*
EXPERIENCE	*We're having a nice time.*
RECEIVE/OBTAIN	*We had a letter today.*
POSSESSION	*They have a big house.*
CHARACTER	*She has a good memory.*
STATES	*I have a headache.*
RELATIONS	*She has six brothers.*
OBLIGATION	*I have (got) to go.*
CAUSE	*She had her hair cut.*
IDIOMS	*I had better go.* *I've had it!*

Power Verb 2

Do

- DO can be a main verb. See table opposite.

- DO is very often an auxiliary verb.
  Do you like coffee? No, I don't.

- DO often replaces another verb.
  I like pasta. So do I.

- DO is often used for emphasis.
  I do love you. Really!

 DO and MAKE

MAKE usually means to create something. *She made a table. He made a cake.*

Apart from the meanings on this page, MAKE is usually the right choice. Make ... *an offer, an excuse, an arrangement, a plan, a mistake, a noise, money* ...

Use/meaning	Example
UNSPECIFIED ACTIVITY	*What are you doing?*
WORK	*He does all the housework.*
PROGRESS PERFORMANCE	*She did very well in her exams.*
BE ENOUGH	*I can't stay long. Will an hour do?*
BE SUITABLE	*This restaurant will do.*
REPLACE ANOTHER VERB	*Go and do (clean) your teeth.* *Have you done (brushed) your hair?*
IDIOMS	*Can you do me a favour?* *It won't do any good.*

Power Verb 3
Be

- BE as main verb is generally used to describe states of affairs – how things are now or generally. See the table opposite.

- BE is also an auxiliary verb, used for progressive verb forms.

  I am working. She has been reading.

- BE is also used to indicate passive forms.

  Smoking is forbidden. The grass has been cut. It was damaged.

Use/meaning	Examples
NOUNS REFER TO SAME THING [NOUN+BE+NOUN]	*Sarah is my boss.*
QUALITY [BE+ADJ]	*He's happy.*
POSITION TIME [BE+ADV]	*He's upstairs.* *They're late.*
EXISTENCE [THERE+BE]	*There's a knife on the table.*
RULE/ORDER ARRANGEMENTS	*Visitors are to leave by ten o'clock.* *We are to be married soon.*

Power Verb 4

Get

- GET has a number of 'basic' meanings. See the table opposite.

- GET can often be used in place of BE in passive constructions – though usually in colloquial language. *I got sent home from school.*
  GET is often used in a reflexive way to talk about things we do to ourselves.

  We got married.

- In British English, *have got* is often used in spoken English in place of *have*, when talking about possession, or in place of *must*.

  They've got a new house. I've got to go now.

Use/meaning	Examples
RECEIVE/OBTAIN	*I've got a new job.*
FETCH	*I'll get the paper.*
BECOME	*We couldn't get warm.*
MOVEMENT	*Get out! Get up!*
START	*Let's get moving!*
CAUSE	*I got her a new job.* *We got him out of prison.* *We got the car serviced.*
PASSIVE MEANING	*I got invited to the party.*
REFLEXIVE	*I got dressed.*

Power Verb 5

Go

- GO has many different uses in English. See the table opposite.

- A common modern colloquial use of GO is to replace *say* when reporting what someone else said. It is <u>not</u> recommended that you use this.

  'What do you want?' I said. And she goes, 'It's nothing to do with you!'

Use/meaning	Examples
LEAVE	*I must go now.*
MOVEMENT	*We went by plane.*
DIRECTION	*The road goes west.*
FINISH	*Has the wine all gone?*
BECOME/CHANGE	*His hair is going grey.*
ACTIVITY	*He went shopping.*
IDIOM	*Things are going well.* *Money doesn't go far these days.*

Review 10

A Replace the verb in italics with *have* or *got*.

1 He *took* a bath.
2 She *fetched* the document from the other room.
3 He *possesses* a wonderful memory.
4 We *have been experiencing* terrible storms.

B *Do* or *make*?

1 Who's .... the cooking tonight?
2 He .... most of his money in banking.
3 I'm sorry, I .... a mistake.
4 Can I help? I'm not .... anything at the moment.

C Which auxiliary: *have*, *be* or *do*?

1 She .... never been to Africa.
2 He .... talking to his father.
3 .... you go to Brazil last year?
4 The project .... never completed.

Irregular verbs

Present	Past	Past participle
be	was	been
beat	beat	beaten
become	became	become
begin	began	begun
bend	bent	bent
bet	bet	bet
bite	bit	bitten
blow	blew	blown
break	broke	broken
bring	brought	brought
build	built	built
buy	bought	bought
catch	caught	caught
choose	chose	chosen
come	came	come
cost	cost	cost
cut	cut	cut
dig	dug	dug
do	did	done
draw	drew	drawn

Present	Past	Past participle
drink	drank	drunk
drive	drove	driven
eat	ate	eaten
fall	fell	fallen
feed	fed	fed
feel	felt	felt
fight	fought	fought
find	found	found
fly	flew	flown
forget	forgot	forgotten
forgive	forgave	forgiven
freeze	froze	frozen
get	got	got
give	gave	given
go	went	gone
grow	grew	grown
hang	hung	hung
have	had	had
hear	heard	heard
hide	hid	hidden
hit	hit	hit
hold	held	held
hurt	hurt	hurt

Present	Past	Past participle
keep	kept	kept
know	knew	known
lay	laid	laid
lead	led	led
leave	left	left
lend	lent	lent
let	let	let
lie	lay	lain
lose	lost	lost
make	made	made
mean	meant	meant
meet	met	met
pay	paid	paid
put	put	put
read	read	read
run	ran	run
say	said	said
see	saw	seen
sell	sold	sold
send	sent	sent
set	set	set
shake	shook	shaken
shine	shone	shone

Present	Past	Past participle
shoot	shot	shot
show	showed	shown
shut	shut	shut
sing	sang	sung
sit	sat	sat
sleep	slept	slept
speak	spoke	spoken
spend	spent	spent
split	split	split
spread	spread	spread
stand	stood	stood
steal	stole	stolen
stick	stuck	stuck
strike	struck	struck
swim	swam	swum
take	took	taken
teach	taught	taught
tear	tore	torn
tell	told	told
think	thought	thought
throw	threw	thrown
wear	wore	worn
win	won	won

Index

Your language

accuse /əkjuːz/
She accused him of stealing the money. _____

achieve /ətʃiːv/
She achieved her objective. _____

act /ækt/
Olivier acted in many great plays. _____

add /æd/
If you add two plus two, you get four. _____

admit /ədmɪt/
I never admit that I'm wrong. _____

adopt /ədɒpt/
The company adopted a new logo. _____

agree /əgriː/
We agreed on a deal. _____

aim /eɪm/
He aimed for promotion. _____

announce /ənaʊns/
The newspapers announced the news. _____

answer /ɑːnsə/
Let me answer that question. _____

Your language

appear /əpɪə/
She appeared in a Hollywood film.
_____

apply /əplaɪ/
He applied for a new job.
_____

argue /ɑːgjuː/
They argue about everything.
_____

arrive /əraɪv/
He was the first to arrive at the party.
_____

ask /ɑːsk/
Can I ask a question?
_____

attend /ətend/
I attended the meeting and gave views.
_____

avoid /əvɔɪd/
The bypass avoids the city centre.
_____

award /əwɔːd/
He was awarded an Oscar.
_____

base on /beɪs ɒn/
The film is based on the novel.
_____

be /biː/
Sally is my boss.
_____

Your language

beat /biːt/
You must play better to beat the others.
_____

become /bɪkʌm/
She became managing director.
_____

begin /bɪgɪn/
The match began at 4 pm.
_____

believe /bɪliːv/
I believe everything you say.
_____

break /breɪk/
Records are broken at the Olympics.
_____

bring /brɪŋ/
Bring a friend with you to the party.
_____

build /bɪld/
Our success is built on Internet sales.
_____

buy /baɪ/
They bought a larger house.
_____

call /kɔːl/
The line's engaged. Can you call later?
_____

can /kæn/
He can swim very well.
_____

Your language

care /keə/
The company cares about its staff.
_____

carry /kæri/
I carried the shopping home.
_____

catch /kætʃ/
The police rarely catch burglars.
_____

cause /kɔːz/
Bad driving caused the accident.
_____

change /tʃeɪndʒ/
He changed his job last year.
_____

cheat /tʃiːt/
She cheated in the exam.
_____

check /tʃek/
I'll just check the figures.
_____

choose /tʃuːz/
He chose to become a doctor.
_____

claim /kleɪm/
I claimed for it on my insurance.
_____

close /kləʊz/
Pubs usually close at 11 pm.
_____

Your language

collect /kəlekt/
Collect my suit from the shop, please.

commit /kəmɪt/
Everybody has committed some crime.

compare /kəmpeə/
You can't compare London with Paris.

complain /kəmpleɪn/
She complained about the poor service.

complete /kəmpliːt/
Complete the form with your details.

continue /kəntɪnjuː/
Let's continue this discussion tomorrow.

control /kəntrəʊl/
The teacher couldn't control his class.

cost /kɒst/
This sofa cost a lot of money.

create /krieɪt/
The new project will create more jobs.

cross /krɒs/
He crossed the road to post my letter.

Your language

cut /kʌt/ _____
We can cut costs by half.

deal /diːl/ _____
We deal with all sorts of people.

decide /dɪsaɪd/ _____
I decided to buy a new car.

demand /dɪmɑːnd/ _____
He demanded a rise in his salary.

deliver /dɪlɪvə/ _____
Will you deliver it to my house?

deny /dɪnaɪ/ _____
He denied he had done wrong.

depend /dɪpend/ _____
It depends on where you live.

design /dɪzaɪn/ _____
This furniture was designed by Chloe.

develop /dɪveləp/ _____
We're developing new products.

die /daɪ/ _____
She died of a heart attack.

Your language

discover /dɪskʌvə/
I have discovered his secret.

discuss /dɪskʌs/
Let's discuss the plans.

do /duː/
He does all the housework.

draw /drɔː/
Let me draw you a map.

drive /draɪv/
I learnt to drive at 18.

drop /drɒp/
She dropped the glass and it broke.

earn /ɜːn/
He earned £80,000 last year.

employ /ɪmplɔɪ/
The company employs many people.

enable /ɪneɪbəl/
His computer enables him to write.

encourage /ɪnkʌrɪdʒ/
Father encouraged me to work hard.

Your language

end /end/
The show must end this week.
_____

enjoy /ɪndʒɔɪ/
Enjoy yourself!
_____

ensure /ɪnʃʊə/
Please ensure the doors are locked.
_____

enter /entə/
She knocked and entered the room.
_____

examine /ɪgzæmɪn/
The police examined her bag.
_____

expect /ɪkspekt/
She's away. I expect she's on holiday.
_____

explain /ɪkspleɪn/
He explained how to use the video.
_____

express /ɪkspres/
You can express your opinion openly.
_____

face /feɪs/
We must face the facts.
_____

fail /feɪl/
I never failed an exam.
_____

Your language

fall /fɔːl/
Prices are falling.

feel /fiːl/
I feel sick.

find /faɪnd/
He couldn't find his keys.

finish /ˈfɪnɪʃ/
I've finished the job.

fit /fɪt/
These trousers don't fit me any more.

fly /flaɪ/
I flew to New York in an executive jet.

follow /ˈfɒləʊ/
They followed the signs.

forget /fəˈget/
I never forget a face.

gain /geɪn/
The baby gained weight regularly.

get /get/
Get out!

Your language

give /gɪv/
I gave her a watch for her birthday. _____

go /gəʊ/
I'm going home. _____

grab /græb/
He grabbed the bag and ran. _____

happen /hæpən/
Something must have happened. _____

hate /heɪt/
She hates violence. _____

have /hæv/
We are having a nice time. _____

hear /hɪə/
I can hear a baby crying. _____

hold /həʊld/
Hold the line. I'll put you through. _____

hope /həʊp/
I hope the new project will succeed. _____

identify /aɪdentəfaɪ/
Nobody could identify the victim. _____

Your language

imagine /ɪmædʒin/
I can't imagine living on a desert island.

    _____

improve /ɪmpruːv/
The financial situation has improved.

    _____

include /ɪnkluːd/
Is service included in the bill?

    _____

increase /ɪnkriːs/
Profits have increased by 20% this year.

    _____

introduce /ɪntrədjuːs/
We introduced a new system.

    _____

invite /ɪnvait/
I wasn't invited to the party.

    _____

join /dʒɔɪn/
They've joined the tennis club.

    _____

keep /kiːp/
I've kept all your letters.

    _____

know /nəʊ/
I know everything about you.

    _____

laugh /lɑːf/
Charlie Chaplin makes me laugh.

    _____

Your language

lead /liːd/
She leads a very interesting life.

learn /lɜːn/
I'm learning Japanese.

leave /liːv/
The plane left on time.

lie /laɪ/
I could lie on a beach all day!

lift /lɪft/
Don't lift that – it's far too heavy.

like /laɪk/
I don't like coffee.

listen /lɪsən/
I'm listening to the radio.

look /lʊk/
We looked at his holiday photos.

lose /luːz/
I went on a diet and lost five kilos.

love /lʌv/
I love popcorn.

Your language

make /meɪk/ _____
He made his debut as Macbeth.

manage /mænɪdʒ/ _____
She manages a large team of employees.

marry /mæri/ _____
We were married in church.

matter /mætə/ _____
Oh I've broken it! – It doesn't matter.

mean /miːn/ _____
What does this word mean?

meet /miːt/ _____
I met Bob for the first time last week.

mention /menʃən/ _____
I was happy to help. Don't mention it.

mind /maɪnd/ _____
I don't mind if we go out or stay in.

miss /mɪs/ _____
She missed the bus.

move /muːv/ _____
Someone has moved my keys!

Your language

name /neɪm/
They named their son John.
_____

need /niːd/
This pasta needs more salt.
_____

notice /nəʊtɪs/
I noticed she was upset.
_____

observe /əbzɜːv/
They observed the situation closely.
_____

obtain /əbteɪn/
She obtained an MBA from Harvard.

offer /ɒfə/
They offered him a much bigger salary.
_____

open /əʊpən/
I opened the letter.

order /ɔːdə/
It wasn't in stock so I ordered it.
_____

pass /pɑːs/
I passed my driving test the first time.
_____

pay /peɪ/
I'll pay by credit card.
_____

Your language

push /pʊʃ/
Push the button for service.
———————

put /pʊt/
I put my keys on the kitchen table.
———————

reach /riːtʃ/
We reached our target easily.
———————

read /riːd/
I read the newspaper every day.
———————

realise /rɪəlaɪz/
I realised I would never be 30 again.
———————

receive /rɪsiːv/
I received three letters this morning.
———————

recognise /rekəgnaɪz/
He's changed – I didn't recognise him.
———————

record /rɪkɔːd/
They always record in the same studios.
———————

reduce /rɪdjuːs/
We should reduce the work force.
———————

reflect /rɪflekt/
The weak Euro reflects the economy.
———————

Your language

reveal /rɪviːl/
She revealed herself at last.
_____

ride /raɪd/
I learnt to ride a bicycle when I was six.
_____

rise /raɪz/
The sun rises every morning.
_____

run /rʌn/
He runs three miles every day.
_____

save /seɪv/
I saved enough to buy a new car.
_____

say /seɪ/
They said that they were coming.
_____

see /siː/
He can't see much without his glasses.
_____

seem /siːm/
She seems very nice.
_____

sell /sel/
Shops don't always sell fresh fruit.
_____

send /send/
She sent me a birthday present.
_____

Your language

share /ʃeə/

We shared expenses equally.

show /ʃəʊ/

Show me an example.

sign /saɪn/

I forgot to sign the cheque.

smile /smaɪl/

She smiles all the time.

sound /saʊnd/

Your trip sounds exciting.

speak /spiːk/

I spoke to the manager about it.

spend /spend/

How much did you spend?

stand /stænd/

There were no seats, so we had to stand.

star /stɑː/

He starred in many Hollywood films.

start /stɑːt/

Start at the beginning.

Your language

stay /steɪ/
I stayed with some friends. _____

stick /stɪk/
He stuck to his position obstinately. _____

stop /stɒp/
The car stopped at the traffic lights. _____

strike /straɪk/
Workers usually strike for more money. _____

suffer /sʌfə/
After the operation, he suffered pain. _____

suggest /sədʒest/
I suggest we begin the meeting. _____

suit /suːt/
That colour doesn't suit you. _____

supply /səplaɪ/
We supply customers all over the world. _____

suppose /səpəʊs/
I suppose he's away. _____

survive /səvaɪv/
He survived a terrible accident. _____

Your language

talk /tɔːk/
We talked about the project.
_____

teach /tiːtʃ/
She taught French in a primary school.
_____

thank /θæŋk/
Thank you for the lovely flowers!
_____

train /treɪn/
An athlete trains several hours a day.
_____

travel /trævəl/
They've travelled round the world.
_____

try /traɪ/
We tried some new Californian wine.
_____

turn /tɜːn/
Turn left at the corner.
_____

understand /ʌndəstænd/
I don't understand spoken French.
_____

use /juːz/
I don't know how to use this computer.
_____

visit /vɪzɪt/
Have you visited Egypt?
_____

Your language

wait /weɪt/
We waited half an hour for a bus. _____

walk /wɔːk/
I walked home. _____

want /wɒnt/
What do you want to do? _____

warn /wɔːn/
I warned you not to walk on the ice. _____

wear /weə/
She was wearing jeans and a T-shirt. _____

welcome /welkəm/
We welcomed the newcomers warmly. _____

win /wɪn/
We won the race easily. _____

wish /wɪʃ/
I wish to make a complaint. _____

wonder /wʌndə/
I wonder where they are. _____

work /wɜːk/
We work eight hours a day. _____

Answers

Review 1
A 1 forgot 2 agree 3 gained 4 suffer 5 believe
B 1 wish 2 decide 3 improved 4 fallen 5 met

Review 2
A 1d; 2a; 3e; 4b; 5c
B 1 lie 2 keep 3 travelled
C 1 I don't mind. 2 I prefer the Brasserie.
    3 I suggest the Bistro.

Review 3
A 1 doesn't fit 2 cost 3 tried 4 refuse
B 1 complained 2 spent 3 pay 4 save

Review 4
A 1 check 2 expect 3 invited 4 understand
    5 obtained
B 1b; 2d; 3a; 4e; 5c

Review 5
A 1 employs 2 produced 3 increased 4 aim
    5 reach
B 1 say 2 expresses 3 ask 4 answer 5 discuss

Review 6

A 1 stop 2 wonder

B 1 has/'s happened 2 wonder 3 depends 4 miss
5 replace

Review 7

A 1 lost 2 dropped 3 prevented 4 laughed
5 started

B 1 Smile 2 add 3 included 4 encouraged
5 run

Review 8

A 1 admitted 2 denied 3 attended 4 signed 5 worried

B 1 warned 2 caught 3 won 4 hear

Review 9

A 1 imagined/have imagined 2 have discovered 3 dies
4 ends 5 make

B 1 awarded 2 entered 3 acts 4 recognised 5 stars

Review 10

A 1 had 2 got 3 has 4 get

B 1 doing 2 makes/made 3 made 4 doing

C 1 has 2 is 3 Did 4 was